Trading

I have had the privileg   y

and have witnessed his   s

book is a testimonial to this inner journey. I am convinced that both men and women of today will benefit from his heart-felt realizations of painstaking self exploration that is rendered so well in a poetic language.

> — **Manisha Roy, Ph.D. Analytical Psychologist,**
> **USA and author of** *Women, Stereotypes and*
> *Archetypes and Bengali Women*

"Trading Armour for a Flower" is a lyrical blend of poems and prose, which explores the nuance of masculinity beyond the conventional gender role and patriarchy. Through intimate reflections, Manish Srivastava has woven a deeper and more liberating meaning of "being masculine" which is capable of greater sensitivity and compassion. This book would be a delightful and insightful reading for many whose thoughts and experiences it echoes.

> — **Dr. Madhukar Shukla,**
> **Professor at XLRI and author of** *Competing through*
> *Knowledge: Building a Learning Organisation*

This is an enthralling and hugely relatable book of verse. Manish has voiced the hidden, unspoken cauldron of a man's feelings in his journey to find himself. His words touched deep places inside.

> — **Sukhvinder Sircar, Founder**
> *Joyous Women: Leadership for Divine Feminine Program*

This is sensitive yet deliberate. Insightful yet provocative. Looks back yet looks ahead. What a master collection of wisdom, sculpted both in poetry and prose. Throughly enjoyable as a nice read as much for the intellectual stimulation.

— Prabir Jha, Former CHRO at
Cipla, Reliance, Tata Motors Ltd

This book speaks from the depths of the heart of every man. Manish has articulated many invisible struggles, unsaid feelings and unconscious hopes. These belong not only to him but to all of us in today's day and age. The poems that spring from his embodied experience shall take you to places that need seeing and healing.

— Abhishek Thakore, International Youth Activist,
Co-founder *Gender Lab and Blue Ribbon Movement*

I want to thank Manish for starting a long due discussion on masculinity. His poetry made me reflect over 70 years of my life as a man. It spoke to the part of me that feels torn between the demands of being soft, emotional and being strong and ruthless. This book raises important questions and brings new hope to masculinity. And at the same time, it could start a conversation among women about their masculine and feminine energies.

— Peter Brunner, Founder
Synchronize-Consult Germany, Business Leader at
Daimler (Mercedes), Sports Coach, Avid Biker

Trading
Armour
for a
Flower

Rise of New Masculine

Manish Srivastava

INDIA · SINGAPORE · MALAYSIA

Notion Press

Old No. 38, New No. 6
McNichols Road, Chetpet
Chennai - 600 031

First Published by Notion Press 2019
Copyright © Manish Srivastava 2019
All Rights Reserved.

ISBN 978-1-64650-972-0

Illustrations by Manish Srivastava

To my parents

Mrs. Vinay Srivastava
Mr. Indra Sen Srivastava

Your unconditional love is the garden
Where I flourish like a flower
Your generosity inspires me
To honour and transcend my armour

You dedicated your life to nourish mine
In your grace I stand, I bloom, I shine!

Gratitude

This book is a mandala. A colourful synthesis of patterns. A temporary sense of completion. An acknowledgement of the journey that brought me here.

I am deeply grateful to my co-travellers:

My loving wife, Sonali Gera, for being my inspiration, my first audience, my editor and co-bearer of my struggles on this ongoing journey.

My dear son, Samay Srivastava, for calling forth my divine feminine & divine masculine and teaching me how to love and play.

My sister Pragya Srivastava and brother Piyush Srivastava, for being gracious listeners and unconditionally supporting my creative pursuits.

My mentors and friends—Vasudevan Alasingachar, Manisha Roy, Arawana Hayashi, Swati Srivastava, Samata Vasisht, Parag Bhargava, Beth Mount, Sukhvinder Sircar, Abhishek Thakore, Sorabh Gupta, Sanjay Dutt, Kiran Gulrajani, Manoj Mone, Silvia Siller, Jagruti Gala, Katrin Kaufer, Kelvy Bird, V. Suresh and Orkide Daniel for their valuable feedback and encouragement in shaping this book.

And all masters, poets, philosophers, artists who have walked this path before me. They have inspired and humbled me. Their timeless wisdom is calling us again on this transforming journey.

Contents

Invitation

Part 1
Threshold of Knowledge

Part 2
Threshold of Love

Part 3
Threshold of Power

Integration

Invitation

He Longs to be Understood

He is either hated or left ignored
Sometimes feared, sometimes disowned
Staring deep in his unhealed wounds
Either way, he is not understood

He is often blamed for aeons of oppression
Or perpetually shamed for overflow of testosterone
Struggling to stand beyond judgements and victimhood
Either way, he is not understood

He is either demonised in feminist rage
Or sacrificed on fronts in glory and praise
Suffering alone in patriarchal falsehood
Either way, he is not understood

He lived exiled in both their hearts
Neither she nor he could claim this part
He now returns from deep, dark woods
Don't deny him, he longs to be understood

When Armour Hurts

Author's Introduction

No man is born free. We are born in an armour. Handed down the generations, carefully crafted by civilisation, and, moulded by societal roles. This armour has been designed to give us pride and protection and keep our kind in a specific order. Some call it "macho-alpha-male". Some call it "patriarchy". All our life we long to grow and inherit our armour.

However, at some stage, our armour starts hurting from within. We long to drink the sun, soak naked in the rain, walk barefoot and dress up in mud and ash. Parts of us want to step out of the armour. Often at the cost of being ridiculed, judged and misunderstood. Outside our armour lies the question that's alive in every man and woman today.

What does it mean to be a man in the 21st Century?

This question is alive in changing roles within families, in women speaking against sexual harassment at work, in feminist discourse, in men's rights movement, in increasing rate of suicide among men and in the intimate conversations that each man has with himself in his lonely quarters.

* * *

I assumed I was a free man and remained almost oblivious, to the privilege and burden of my armour, till I became a father, in 2012. While fatherhood brought many joys and gifts to my life, it also brought me face-to-face with the old saying: "It takes a village to raise a child!"

When I looked around, all known models of "village" were based on the old patriarchal social systems. Dividing men and women in gendered roles with an alpha male in the centre and women in the background. Creating inner conflicts. Making men burdened and exhausted as providers and protectors. Making women shadowed and exploited as mere child-bearers and caretakers. Both genders feeling stuck while projecting their anger on each other. Either-way, its children, who suffered the most. Being raised as prototypes of the same pattern that their gender belonged to.

Around this time, I left a stable career with a leading corporation and started working as a freelancer, somehow balancing parenting and consulting. Often I was the only man showing up at my son's kindergarten and household discussions. While some women glorified me as a super-dad, my work colleagues, including a woman CEO, ridiculed me for being "lost in domestic life at the prime of his career". At one hand, I became a misfit in men's social world and on the other, I felt judged and unaccepted by most women. I wondered if I was disrupting their power or powerless narrative.

Stepping out of our traditional masculine armours also meant stepping into deep inner conflict. It was as if, parts of me were at war with each other. One part wanted to create a new egalitarian community for my child, while other part enjoyed the convenience of old patriarchy. One part could not relate to other men who lived macho-alpha-male paradigm, while the other part was envious of the power and control they had on their lives. At times I felt there were many "me's" living in the house. Who provoked who was unpredictable and scary. Deep down, I was being torn and dragged into darkness.

* * *

2012, something happened in India that left a scar we may never recover from. A young girl was brutally gang-raped in a moving bus and left to die on the roadside. The whole country was shocked and enraged. Women and men marched in protest. Our government acted helplessly and named the victim "Nirbhaya" (fearless one) while she died a painful death.

For nights I could not sleep. How could a public tragedy be so painful personally? I could feel the intense pain, suffering and helplessness of the victim who was raped. I could sense the collective anger of women. And somehow, I also felt responsible for the rapist. As if I had created him. I could see the systemic oppression that he went through and yet I could not forgive him for the gruesome act of inhumanity. My legs shivered as Nirbhaya episode touched the raw nerve of repressed sexuality, oppression and violence within me. But, I had no forum to express and explore my innermost feelings. Most men avoided this conversation. Women had no space to accommodate any emotion other than shared-anger for all patriarchy and those six rapists in particular.

Fortunately, a few months later, at a Non-Violent Communication (NVC) conference, facilitators organised an open dialogue between men and women. They allowed both genders to explore their locked emotions after Nirbhaya tragedy. I felt high intensity and tinge of judgement when women, standing in the outer circle, asked: "And how do you men feel about women being raped, abused and exploited!?" I was sitting on the floor among men. It was heartbreaking to see men opening their hearts, sharing their fear, pain, anger, shame and their struggle with sexuality and rage. Somehow, the process gave us the courage to name the raw nerve I was experiencing all the while.

Most women in the room said that they did not expect men to be so open, vulnerable and honest. As we walked out, I overheard some women saying that "Its hard to believe that men felt like this. They aren't like real men in the real world. Perhaps, they are trained to speak in NVC language."

Once again, I felt that a part of me, a part of masculine, is not understood or trusted by women or men. I wondered why vulnerable aspects of a man are so unacceptable. While it's the part, that holds the potential to nurture and heal humanity.

* * *

2012 was also significant, cause, this was the year when Mayans predicted that "the world would come to an end!"

I happened to share my inner struggle with my friend, Sukhvinder Sircar, who has been working, with groups of women[1], on integrating their inner feminine and masculine energies. She helped me realise that my struggle was part of a universal phenomenon. Maybe, what Mayans had predicted was— "in 2012, old world order would come to an end!". The old order of patriarchy that was driven by wounded, ego-centric masculine was ending. It had created a world that suppressed the feminine, dishonoured the woman and exploited nature.

Beyond our social constructs of man and woman, each one of us has feminine and masculine energy within. Both these energies can manifest as divine (holistic, sane, serving the whole) or as wounded (manipulative, insecure, damaging others). When masculine & feminine integrate as divine and whole, within any man or woman, we have a complete human, capable of loving-protecting, creating-dissolving, leading-following, simultaneously. However, when they are wounded or out of balance, we have violence, conflicts, disasters and diseases.

---

1   More information on Sukhvinder Sircar's work is available at www.facebook.com/Joyouswoman/

When I looked at these energies within me, I discovered a long-disempowered feminine and a deeply-wounded masculine. Wounded masculine is often manifested as macho-alpha-male—invincible, tough, aggressive, commanding and controlling. However, these traits are not limited to men. Even modern women have been sporting it more aggressively than their counterparts.

Perhaps, these traits were of great importance to our ancestors while they travelled across wild and wastelands, settled in harsh environments, confronted the unknown of death and disasters. Their old pattern still lives in our collective muscle memory as patriarchy. It has helped men manage the world for many centuries. It also created a grossly unfair divide between the genders. Most women suffered. A few found their own way to empowerment. They organised themselves and created a sense of solidarity. Their collective movement strengthened. Men, on the top of patriarchal world order, remained insensitive or ignorant to the world they were creating.

However, men who were not propagators of patriarchy were lost. They were neither fully familiar with their divine feminine nor had empowered their divine masculine. They suffered the battle between sexes. The Red Pill movie[2] reflects a part of this suffering by highlighting wounded masculinity of feminist movements.

---

2   The Red Pill. Documentary film. Directed by Cassie Jaye (2016). www.theredpillmovie.com

This pattern repeats as fractals in institutions and global social system as well. The social, ecological & spiritual divides[3] that we are confronted with are a manifestation of ego-centric wounded masculine energy. Few in power, control all resources to feed their self-interest. The world now is seeking for a new eco-consciousness that integrates masculine & feminine, yin & yang, profits & people, economic growth & ecological sustainability.

Indian mythology and wisdom traditions honour the integration of divine masculine and divine feminine as *Ardhanarishvara:* a composite androgynous form of Shiva and Shakti. It is the seed of Supreme Being that lives within each man and woman. Our current challenges are perhaps a set-up for the manifestation of Ardhanarishvara.

As Mayans and other wisdom traditions foresaw, a new world order that integrates and celebrates both feminine and masculine is rising now in every heart. Part of this work is left up to men to honour the new masculine energy that is beyond alpha and that redefines the patriarchal world order.

Over the last seven years, my quest for discovering my new masculine energy has intensified. I got inspired by Mythopoetic Men's Movement[4] and work of Poet Robert Bly[5]. It gave me the courage to set sail in the

---

3   Scharmer, C.O., & Kaufer, K. (2013). Leading from the emerging future: From Ego-System to Eco-System Economies. San Francisco: Berrett-Koehler Publishers, Inc.

4   https://en.wikipedia.org/wiki/Mythopoetic_men's_movement

5   http://www.robertbly.com

uncharted waters of the divine masculine. Soon, I met other men who were on a similar quest[6]. My friends, colleagues, coaching clients, workshop participants, blog readers and sometimes complete strangers shared their longing to heal the man within themselves. Some of us gathered in circles to open our hearts and explore this new energy.

My journey is ongoing, and so is the rise of the new masculine. This book is a synthesis of my explorations. Though stated in the first person, this book is neither an autobiographical narrative of people in my life nor a political commentary on gender divides. My life and work context have helped me to reflect on the inner dimensions of my psyche. Most of these poems are inspired by fragments of my dreams, active imagination and contemplative embodiment practices. Captured as reflections and poetry, this book opens some windows of my heart. I invite you to look within and explore: What windows are opening in your heart? What's wounded within? Where are you seeing the new masculine rising in your life?

Masculinity is the energy living within both men and women. And therefore this book is relevant to both. I hope my fellow men find their resonance and new questions. I hope my fellow women also discover

---

6   I am grateful to Sorabh, Sanjay, Kiran and Abhishek for co-creating space where men could reflect and deepen their journey to new masculine

how they respond to the new masculine energy within themselves and with those they relate to. Together, we may illuminate this field and help other men and women to step out of our armours. As poet Rumi invited us 800 years ago:

"Out beyond ideas of wrongdoing and rightdoing, there is a field. I'll meet you there."

Emerging Map of this Journey

Each poem and reflection in this book has been gathered, over seven years, in different spaces—journals, cell-phone, emails, paper napkins, boarding passes etc. Often it started with some intense experience of being a man in this dynamic social world. Then the subtle, unconscious aspect of that experience manifested as a dream, a visual flash, some synchronous event, an accident. I took some fragments of these dreams & images to the contemplative practice of active imagination[7] or embodiment[8]. Some were ripe and ready. Either way, they midwifed a poem.

When they all came together, they revealed their first pattern—Nine themes or chapters of my journey to the new masculine. Once, I compiled the

---

7   I learnt dream analysis and active imagination while being in Jungian Analysis and attending open courses on Jungian Psychology over a year at C.J. Jung Institute, Boston https://cgjungboston.com

8   I am grateful to Social Presencing Theatre, a movement-based contemplative art form that has helped me embrace and articulate the subtle, complex and non-verbal aspects of human experience. https://www.presencing.org/aboutus/spt

first draft, I saw another pattern. Nine themes could be organised under 3 meta-themes with 3 chapters each. It seems my ongoing journey of healing my wounded masculine has gone through 3 thresholds with 3 moves each.

The threshold of knowledge requires us to overcome three past conditionings of wounded masculine—righteousness, ignorance & control. As we cross this threshold, we are gifted with insight and openness to face our deep wounds.

The threshold of love is an invitation to embrace the deep wounds of betrayal, sexuality & abandonment. It opens our heart and gifts us with empathy and longing to serve.

Finally, **the threshold of power** calls us to serve the world by stepping into our authentic sources of power. This includes—the power to be free from institutional slavery, the power to rule, and, the power to dissolve.

The patterns of this kaleidoscope may be endless. I hope you discover your own. For now, enjoy this.

Who am I beyond the scriptures
Picking pieces
Lost in long trails of civilisation
A relay my ancestors braved for ages
And the earth that preserved the map
Hidden in depths of my body

Preparatory Footnote[9]

---

9 **Dear Unconscious**
I know you are threatened by my creative expression
Ready to do anything to stop
Fear of being vulnerable is understandable
Please brace yourself
We will get thru this anyways!

Part 1

Threshold of Knowledge

Overcoming Past Conditionings

Trading Armour for a Flower
Journey into the Dark Forest
Deep Dive in the Burning Sea

The first step in our journey to the new masculine is crossing the threshold of knowledge, guarded by the demons of past conditioning about manhood & masculinity. Past conditionings are widely held beliefs that keep us prisoned in a wounded masculine state. Men have championed these habitual patterns and women sometimes imitate them at the cost of their native feminine wisdom. These are the mental chains that hold us from overcoming our ignorance and liberating our true self. Three most pervasive past conditionings are self-righteousness, self-ignorance, and, self-control.

Self-righteousness: "I am right"—Within us lies a deep need for self-righteousness that immediately divides our world into right vs wrong, black vs white, pure vs impure, good vs bad etc. It is at the heart of all racial, religious or gender divides. And the birthplace of all "isms". Leaving each one of us lonely and burdened, protecting our little ego-castles. So many wars have been fought, and so many lives sacrificed over righteousness. The compelling tribal need to justify our historic right is the source of all communal violence. Men have been both perpetrator and disposable victims of the same. The new masculine calls us to let go of this divide and embrace our own rightdoings & wrongdoings. In doing so, we experience humanity within ourselves and in all being. We trade our armours for flowers of acceptance and gratitude.

Chapter 1, "Trading Armour for a Flower" wonders what may happen when we let go of the past conditioning of self-righteousness.

Self-ignorance: "I know it all"—Emerging from some deep distrust of unknown, men created a strong belief that nothing is true unless proven logically. This has lead to significant progress in scientific thought. However, it has also held us from accessing our own vulnerability and inner knowing. We see so many men on top of their institutional pyramid who just can't admit their ignorance or look within their own mess. They neither listen nor leverage the wisdom of collective and end up creating further disaster. Most famines and national crises are results of such "we-know-it-all" leadership. New masculine energy invites us to start from the position of "not-knowing" and look within our own darkness and blindspots. When we dissolve all our references, structures, labels, and, frameworks, we become available to the native wisdom of the collective.

Chapter 2, "Journey into the Dark Forest", invites us to embrace our ignorance and step into the unknown aspects of our own psyche.

Self-control: "I can't look vulnerable"—For how long have we told our boys that they can't cry? Growing up as boys and men, we have to tradeoff our sensitiveness and sadness. This probably served the community to make men disposable assets for wars and trade. But it had severe consequences.

The more we resist our emotions, the more its dark-side persists. If suppressed within, it becomes a source of increasing heart attacks, depression and suicides among men. If expressed without acceptance, it destroys the world with its unpredictable wounded masculine rage. When we dive deep within our melancholy and madness, we start feeling the pain and suffering of those we serve.

Chapter 3, "Deep Dive in the Burning Sea" is an exploration of the unacknowledged sadness and rage we feel within.

Overcoming past conditioning is the first step of courage and clarity. When we step beyond our self-righteous, known and safe ego-castle, we receive the gifts of self-awareness & freedom. We smell the free, fresh breeze and feel the tenderness of a young sapling. We become open to diverse perspectives and ready to take the next journey—to meet our deep wounds—a field that lies beyond the dichotomy of right-wrong, that is unknown and emotionally messy.

1

Trading Armour for a Flower

Men were raised to fight
Denied of their own inner light
Sacrificing themselves for tribal pride

He is letting go of the archaic conditioning—
the compelling need to be right

He is returning to his core
Trading his armour
For a flower

Warrior at heart,
Champion of humanity
He rises again!

Where Past Became a White Butterfly

A compelling need to be right
Sometimes comes to compensate
Years of being wronged

A compelling right to prove our pride
Sometimes comes to cover-up
Years of shame for loosing the same

A compelling desire to assert our identity
Sometimes comes to reclaim
Many lifetimes lost in shadow

Do we really need to walk all the way back
In our long, faded, complex history
To undo those wrongdoings

Can we sleep tonight and
Wake up in a field
Where past became a white butterfly

Self Righteousness of Hurt

Why do we nurture hurt
Like a prized possession
In our bedrooms

What rank or privilege
Can one memory
Of being humiliated ages ago, bring

What hope of revenge or reconciliation
Has contracted our ego
To withstand, forever of suffering

Why do we feel so right
To lock our own bodies in chains of hatred
And throw the keys away

Holding on to a broken raft
Build on painful memories
In the middle of a vast sea of love

When all Arrows are Gone

One moment I lie on my back, wondering
the endless sky above and the apparent insignificance
Of our existence

Next moment I shoot an arrow, chasing
the endless horizon. Vision focussed
Till it's very very end

I jump on my feet, dancing
a tribal celebrating. Heart still sad and knows
It's nothing but an old ritual!

When all arrows are gone
I return to the bow
Hanging loyally on my shoulder

What's at the Heart of Your Heart?

The race to be better is not making sense anymore
The need to win accolades is fading faster than ever
The point I wanted to prove all my life
Has fallen prey to amnesia

Who am "I"?
A rapid de-construction is on
The witness is getting dissolved
Who will tell the story
Who needs it anyways

Drop the number game
That story of 'significance'
Has been preceded by 'in'

Now, look at me and tell me
What's at the heart of your heart?

Given that life is pointless and death is certain
How would you like to hang on here for?
What if the treasure chest we guarded all our life
Is bottomless!

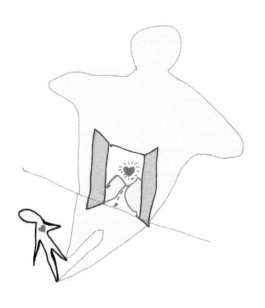

2

Journey into the Dark Forest

His kind has been a champion of logos
Celebrating culture over nature
And order over chaos

He feels the pain of separation from known
And knows the cost of not stepping into the unknown
Wanderer lives in his blood
He has now responded to the call

To the deep, dark forest within
He marches again!

Invitation from the Unknown

Just a few inches below
The well-formed and informed
Lies a free flow of life

Dance between is and isn't
Self-creating, self-destroying
Dark river of bright light

Patterns of playful paradoxes
A sangam of past and future
Timeless, fragile, fresh illusion

If you dare to tear open
The facade of known
The flow of unknown will fill you

Breath in life
Breath out self
Take a dip, dissolve!

Men Need to Travel

Was man ever designed to be a settler?
The hunter, gatherer, wanderer, warrior
Lives deep within him

Before his children learnt to walk,
Beds were made, or the sun dried the dew drops
He packed his bags and responded to the call

Tired, he longs to rest
But, a new invitation awaits from within
Unknowness engulfs his heart

Expert at charting the world out there
He is still a novice to his inner
No map, no guide, only an intense longing

Men need to travel
To find something
To lose something

Old gene knows,
Its never going to be the same again
Sadness wells up…and settles

Unreasonable Calls

Some calls have no reason at all
Some calls come from beyond
Some messengers have no idea either

Sometimes, legs know better than the map
Hands work faster than the brains
Back is more alive than the heart

Sometimes, silence does more speaking
A new world is unlocked by a soft "yes"
It does not matter where it leads

Sometimes, surrendering demands more courage
Not knowing asks for more wisdom
Distancing requires more love

Sometimes there is no ground to step on to
Yet, all that matters is
The first step!

Living on the Edges

It's only on the edges
Vastness reveals itself
You don't know the sea
Till you meet the shore

Depth begins with shallow
Thresholds are worlds too
Where yours, end
And the new one awaits

Edges are doors, honour them
They come again and again
They're the only safe spaces of life
Some souls live there, forever

A warrior stands
Aware of his insignificance to the matters of land
In awe of the magnificence of the sea
Other end is far, unknown, uncharted

3

Deep Dive in the Burning Sea

Men have been at the mercy
Of their own anger and melancholy
Suppressed within or blown outwardly
Either way disastrous

He dived in the volcano from its very head
Letting it burn everything that was long-held
Till a single streak of white light remained
He then fell into the deep sea of sorrow
Sinking to the very end

Bathed in primordial well
He surfaces again!

A Million Small Irritations

Build together into a cloud of hatred and anger
Unspoken, they multiplied
Floating aimlessly, creating restlessness
Blurring the vision, blocking the light
Till one day, they precipitated
Altogether, at one point, one place, one person
Outburst!!!

A storm ended
Leaving disaster – an uncalled-for silence
Neither the sky nor the earth
Neither the rain nor the drenched
Neither the oppressor nor the oppressed
Knows— why did this happen?

They were just tools
The parts that played on behalf of

A million small irritations!
Who are you?
Little deviations from my idea of how the world ought to be
Little disconnects in values
Little voids of needs unmet
Little thought of anger, hatred, violence

A million small irritations!
Where do you come from?
Out beyond my personal journaling
Floating free in the sky
Having power and potent to precipitate
On me or others
Through me or through others
Leaving us both helpless creators of emotional storms

Oh, how I wish, to be an autumn tree!

Sliding into Deep Womb of Sadness

Once we have scaled the mountains of anger,
And crossed the edges of fear,
Sometimes, we slide into an unfamiliar valley
Of sadness and grief

A low lowland,
Long, stretched and seemingly endless
It's here, the wise men once walked
and said "dukha hai" / "life's suffering"

Surrendering shows us a way to true love
For sadness surfaces our deepest longings
Our most dreadful losses
Melting all armours that protected self from Self
And precipitating into tears
Till our soul is bare naked

Then, for the first time in life, we experience
The weight of our bones
Like woods piled for the final journey
It's in this purposelessness
Life reveals its true Self
The beauty of ordinary and impermanence

Words dissolve in the dark canvas of life
Earth cracks open
Sliding us into the womb of healing
And rebirthing us in a meadow of love

But that's not the story tonight
Tonight we sleep quietly
In the quilt of sadness
And it's unbearable cosiness

That Intimate Feverish Night

100.7 degree Fahrenheit
Heat on my forehead
Pain all over my joints
Sedative breaths.
I lie quietly wrapped in my warmth
There is a degree of comfort in illness!

Thoughts are returning from lost wars
Dissolving unwillingly into the body
Few centimetres below my skin
Is raging heat!

Is fever an alternate release
Of what the mind can't fathom
The shadow rejects
Of repressed freedom, love, sexuality

Bluish-green vibrations rise between my legs
A breathing volcano of raw animality
Seductive, ruthless, unforgiving current
Hitting my throat and shaking my torso

This turbulence has meaning
Something is crumbling
Things that I identified with and gave power to
Leaving within an unexplained shiver

Just below my burning diaphragm
Bubbles turn into fearful butterflies
Few inches deep in my abdomen
I feel pain and deep hurt
Many memories shoot up like a firework
Tears roll down my eyes
Carrying old stories
Of hurt and denial
Of falling or failing in love

As the night gives way to dawn,
Pain settles in deep silence
Events happen outside at their own free will
I witness it from some deep place
Like a monk in a cathedral
Watching a firefighter flying above tall buildings

It's vulnerable still yet safe
Safe in knowing that it's all vulnerable anyways

Apparent Pointlessness of Everything

Heart is tender, breathing slowly
Ears hear the clock ticking
Gap between two seconds is palpable
Loud sound of silence in the darkness of night

With every breath
Painful memories of many years are inhaled
And exhaled…
This body is too fragile to resist

Walking barefoot on the shore of sadness & regrets
Refusing to take a dip
Footprints appear and dissolve
The purpose of life hangs in the evening sky
Dispersed pointlessly like white clouds

Burdens of responsibilities
Cages of traditions
Seductions of progressive life
Deception of vanity in the skin of love
And chains by deep, deep fear

Gap between the seconds gets longer
Carrying few lifetimes

I stare at the space in between
The significance of the rising sun
is getting lost in the pointlessness of the dark
Distant voices of loved ones
Are dissolving in silence

Heart opens up again
like a terrace after a night storm
Tender, wet, there!

Part 2

Threshold of Love

Healing Deep Wounds

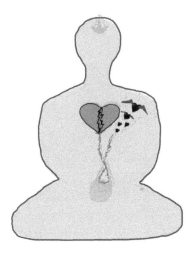

Embracing Rudra and Kali
Dancing Naked with the Wild Women
Standing for the Child

As we prepare to journey beyond the known, safe and habitual patterns, our vulnerable heart brings us face to face with our old wounds of betrayal, shame and abandonment. Much early in our growing up, these wounds created unconscious patterns that keep playing in our current relationships. They shadow our capacity to enjoy the present and appreciate the beauty that lies within us and within all creations. We must walk back to the sources where these wounds come from and heal.

Wounds of Betrayal and an unresolved battle between masculine and feminine. These two divine forces of nature needed space between them for the creation and gave birth to the inseparable dichotomy of Earth-Sky, Adam-Eve, Rudra-Kali, Prakruti-Purush, Ying-Yang. When they first separated, they left a wound on each other. Any separation, seen from only one side often feels like a betrayal. This battle is played a million times within each of us and projected on our closest relationships.

At the societal level, this wound is manifested as a war between angry feminist and insensitive patriarch. Ranging from sexist jokes, workplace discrimination, passive manipulation to gross violence. Gender conflicts are only a surface expression of deep wounds of betrayal that both men & women feel within themselves and with each other.

Whether as a victim or as a perpetrator, it is a call for men to look within. We must meet the feminine on the ground and rise together beyond the gender and role divides. We must integrate the masculine and feminine within each heart.

Chapter 4, "Embracing Rudra and Kali", reflects on the inner conflicts between masculine and feminine played in our intimate relationships.

Wounds of Shame and a deep longing to embrace our sexuality. Story of our civilization is a story of culture taking over nature. The rapid urbanization of our natural world mirrors our attempts to control rawness and passion of our inner world. We created civilised social order and morality that repressed and shamed sexual expression. However, our unattended carnal desires manifested in the dark world of pornography, prostitution and rape-culture. Men, in particular, are most vulnerable to this divide. Feeding the same as unconscious consumers or conscious exploiters. Even those who err on the right side of sexual morality end up living a life lacking creativity, passion and ecstasy.

Chapter 5, "Dancing Naked with the Wild Women", is an invitation to embrace our sensual self and live a shame-free life with love and pure joy.

Wounds of Abandonment and deep sadness of the lost inner-child. Somewhere early in our biography, we abandoned our inner child. The trials of growing up left no space for child-like innocence, curiosity and love. Yet, the child-in-us survives and longs to reconnect.

When we disconnect from our inner child, it manifests as apathy towards the suffering of children all over the world. The image of a dead toddler on Greece coast, or news of 100s of girls being kidnapped and raped in Africa, is a reflection of adults who lost their sensitivity and innocence. Look closer, and you will find a story of abandoned childhood and missing fathers felt by most men of our generation.

Chapter 6, "Standing for the Child", calls upon men to nurture their inner child and grow up as responsible adults. In spite of our woundedness, we need to stand together in service of all children of the future.

The only way to go past the deep wounds is to enter in them and feel them fully. When we feel into the roots of our betrayal, shame and abandonment, we dissolve the patterns of blame, shame and loneliness. The threshold of vulnerability honours us with the gift of self-love. Our heart opens up to relate with others and their sufferings.

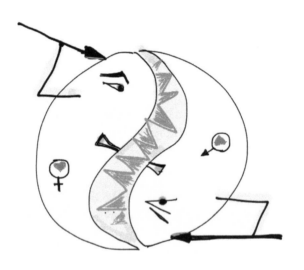

4

Embracing Rudra and Kali[10]

He has been to many wars
Yet it's the matter of the heart
That rips him apart

The revengeful feminine and crushing masculine
Terrifying tandav, danced from eternity
Battle of sexes, for redemption and equality
When will the ball stop?
Why does Shiva lay on feet of Kali?

He has embraced his Rudra and Kali
Still trembling
He opens his heart again!

---

10 Shiva and Shakti together represent the divine masculine and
divine feminine energies in Hindu mythology. Rudra is the
fierce, warrior form of Lord Shiva. Kali is the most powerful
and ferocious form of Goddess Shakti. When Kali is enraged
and uncontrollable, only way Shiva could pacify her and bring
her back is by laying on her feet.

Deep Wounds

The one raging ferociously
In the crowded streets
Riding a wild beast
Bathed bare in dark blood
Swinging the double-edged sword
Slashing heads and hearts around
Screaming anger

She is deeply wounded
All she longs for is respect

The one thumping chest
Racing fiercely in rage
Breathing fire, spewing ash
Uprooting the foundation
Annihilating his own creation
Ripping out his heart
Roaring cry

He is deeply wounded
All he longs for is acceptance

Entanglement

A knife stuck in depths of the heart
Neither does it comes out
Nor let the heart die

Maybe, it's scared of the bloody shower
Piercing was easier
Killing calls for a much bigger heart

Or maybe, its love that keeps them both alive
Pain does have its sweetness
And wounds also give life

Witness only sympathises, from a safe distance
Wondering, why couldn't they learn
Another way to express love?

Aftermath of Everyday Cyclones

As cyclone settles
The aftermath of destruction prevailed

Some parts of me were exiled or evacuated,
Some confronted, struggled and died
Some survived
With shock, grief and pain in their eyes

The violence of nature is massive on scale
The violence of our conversations is no less

Why do we choose our bedroom
to workout lifetime of unresolved issues

Why do I find your rawness, irresistible, only after,
Rage burns the mask and tears washes the facade

It only takes a night of emotional tides
To destroy what was built over the years

Are cyclones absolutely necessary for evolution?

Unfair

Someday, when we cross the veil of life
When they declare us dead
Something is us may still survive

In that brief moment of eternity
We may find ourselves in each other
Like keys of the grand piano
Co-producing the music called life

The father, the mother, the spouse
Even the children
The in-laws, out-laws, maids, masters
Lovers and heartbreaks
All those intimate longings or betrayals
Would come to see us off
As our reflections in the cosmic mirror
Fellow petals of the same flower

Will there be time to seek forgiveness
For the walls, we built against ourselves
Can we call life unfair
For not knowing this divine truth earlier

Intimate Loneliness

Sometimes, in the middle of my loneliness,
I am full

I don't need any companionship
Your distant presence across the room,
Is the highest service you can do,
To me and to yourself

Sometimes, I can see through the facade of relationships
Pointlessness of love
Overrated fear of solitude
Handicap of dependency

Sometimes, neither I nor you, need each other
It's the habit that continues
The "I love you" that has no meaning
The "go away" that's so intimate

Sometimes, I feel so secure
I don't need to reciprocate to your love
There is nothing except the sound of silence
You and I, dissolve in the same backdrop

In those times,
I fall intensely in love with you
Your whole solo-self meets mine
In our aloneness, we are together
Intimate, inseparable

5

Dancing Naked with the Wild Women

Pure raw desires, ousted and shamed
Objectified at the edges of civilisation
Morally bound to rituals of procreation

He has broken his chains of shame
Held the wild woman naked in his arms
Kissed her to ecstasy

Intoxicated with intimacy
He dances again!

Lost in the Labyrinth of Sex

Sex,
Why is it so exotic?
Placed in a labyrinth
With the price tag of social control at every corner

Shame,
A tool of patriarchy
Civilising and enslaving the raw and wild
Into the circus of mankind

Morality,
Manipulating nature's song into an uncontrollable rage
Denying her pleasure
Turning him into a savage

Men,
Prisoners of their own structures
Torn between mind and body
Stoned if they break free
Cursed if they don't

Women,
Unconsciously colluded in this game
Living in an illusionary pride
The baits who celebrated the catch
Who keeps the key to the chastity lock, anyways?

Marriage,
Reduced to an institution that turns carnal into civilised
A battlefield for wounded ancestral pride
An unmet longing for a sacred union
Between two souls still stuck at adulthood rites

Running Between the Raindrops

All my life, I have been running
Between the raindrops

Sometimes they turn into a hailstorm
Sometimes they fall like soft snowflakes
Never have I allowed them to touch me
So precise is my escapism

"Not my call"
I heard my fear saying
"Nothing would change"
My intellect rationalised

But, the child within,
The long exiled warrior
The passionate lonely lover
The dethroned king
All of them, all of them, nodded their heads,
in grief yet compassionate disappointment

She just wants to soak in rain
Bare her breast
And cry out loud in thunderstorm

Oh my wildness
Where did I lose you
in this civilised progression?

Man and Shame

Man met Nature in the woods

"Wow", he said,
"How shamelessly you display
    your most attractive and seductive parts"

Nature smiled and asked,
"And I am surprised,
    why do you feel so shameful and secretive
    about your deepest pleasures?"

Man's hand reached his groin to ensure its covered

A deer passed by,
Naked and beautiful
She said,
    "Hey man, aren't you part of nature too?"

Man sighed,
"Oh Deer, I wear many clothes,
    even when I am naked!"

The Sacred Arousal

Sitting naked, on the edge of a cliff
Looking upwards
Holding two golden drum sticks
Shaped like sensual snakes
The sky is a big drum, I am playing

Rain clouds are dancing like mad
Sea is rising to applause
Earth is yawning in ecstasy
Trees have their leaves erected
And flowers are opening-up
Inviting the first drops of rain
Forest is swinging its head in unison
Rivers are going wild
And all the animals. All of them, including me,
are experiencing—a sacred arousal

Madness, love, surrender and joy
Like never before
Can you hear the beats,
And feel spring in your feet?
Dum damadum dum dum dum

Butterfly Tattoo on Your Lower Back

When I see your butterfly tattoo
Beautifully placed on your lower back
My imagination instantly goes wild
To explore your whole body
Your voluptuous buttocks
Soft navel
Pleasure between your legs

This uncontrollable force within me
Is the purest feeling I ever had
I know your tattoo is not an invitation
And I won't knock your door
But I can't deny the deep desire in me
The urgency to merge in you
Skin to skin
Part to part
Breath to breath

It was never taught to me in any order
Nor is it in my culture
It's some very very old gene pool
Or maybe the divine garden itself

I don't know why you chose that spot
Your beauty and sensuality brings me to the edge
Of my bondage civilization
Wild tides of testosterones rising in rebellion

May I take another look
And steal a glimpse of you, your tattoo
And it's sensual geography
Can I carry it to my cave
Where I build sculptures
From the beauty I collect through the day

Will I be called a thief, a pervert or an artist
Will you forgive me for this plagiarism
For I am forbidden to tell you that I am sexually aroused
And its nothing to do with romance or reverence

6

Standing for the Child

Whenever the father sky thundered upon the earth
It's the child that got crushed
Ego has long justified the destruction, but
Who will answer those hopeful eyes?

He walked down the broken lane
To his old childhood home
Where she lived below the rubble
He vowed to never let her suffer again

For the future of his world
He takes a stand!

When will Father be Home?

Standing, sustaining, resilient
Absolute refusal to give up
In the face of soul-less trauma
We are the earth
We receive, bear, uphold!

    "but for how long?"
    the child turned to the mother—

    "O, mother!
    When will father be home?"
    Sky is so vast and ruthless,
    Dropping bombs, indiscriminately
    Does father-sky, care for us mother?"
    Can he see us, the children?"

Mother took a deep breath—
"My child!
I will nurture you
Sky is but a skin on my vastness & depth
From the crack of the dawn
To the darkest hour of the night
I will hold you"

"For, those who invade the sky are my children too
Lost, arrogant, hurting
One day they too will land
Gently or crashing
that's their journey!
You, my child, will thrive!"

"Why do we suffer, mother?"

The innocence and truth in the child's voice
was unbearable
Mother just looked
with deep, sad, teary eyes
Feeling violated yet powerful
She kissed on her forehead

A Void Deep in My Heart

After I had championed the ways of adulthood
And earned my place in big castles and bright cities
I hit a void, deep in my heart
A void that all my worth could not fill
A void that would consume my every bit

One day, I dared to look deep within
To find a familiar, unkempt, wild track
My mind shivered, but my heart could not resist the call
Legs knew this path
I walked and walked and walked
Till the deep woods gave its way to a clearing
Wildflowers, fluttering butterflies, blue sky

On a rock next to the stream
Lied a little boy, 5 years old
Whispering to the passing clouds

How long, how long, have I left him alone?
My throat choked, my mouth dried
I walked closer and sat next to him

He sensed my arrival
"you are back?"
"yes"… I whispered

He rolled onto his belly, looking straight in my eyes
Innocence kept alive for many lifetimes
Tear-marks still fresh on his cheeks
My heart broke, I cried
"I am sorry, I left you alone
I was so busy catching up with adult life"

"Do you like me?" he asked
My head sank
"I was ashamed of you… you were so small and weak…"

"But you were big… ?" he wondered
A fact, a puzzle this little heart struggled for all these years
"…yes, I was. I am so sorry…
I did not protect you when they came…"

A tear rolled down his cheek
I could feel the pain in my chest
He picked a broken blade of grass and nodded
"…"
A simple gesture with power to accept years of wrongdoing
I held his face in my palms
"I want to walk with you… back to the castle
And live there forever.
I promise you, I will never leave you alone!"

He smiled as if it was yesterday
And jumped and climbed over my shoulders
We crossed the meadow and walked into the rainbow

A Child Suffering Anywhere is Yours

I don't care whether you were responsible
for that refugee crisis or not
That child lying dead on the shore
Is yours!

I don't give a damm for the million years of sufferings
your kind went through
I dare you not to raise your hand on this innocent soul
For she is divine!

I don't want to know what your psychologist told you
about your unresolved childhood issues
Now that you are an adult
All these children in the world look up to you!

Your pain in this relationship might be unbearable
and must you walk out for your self-respect
But I challenge you to grow up and protect
The innocence of the little one longing for your love!

Adulthood is a responsibility
A call for higher leadership
A capacity to sit unresolved with our pain and past
A willingness to surrender self for the children!

The world is done with adolescents
Captured in egotist old bones
We need nurturing souls
Gardeners for a new realm!

Child and the Caged Tigress

Restless like a caged tigress
Cage not big enough to withhold my roar
Rage intense enough to annihilate the zoo

Breathing heavily
Claws on concrete
When will that be?
When will that be?

A child amused at my presence
His innocence is somehow cooling me
Something weird, Something mine

Part 3

Threshold of Power

Reclaiming Inner Source

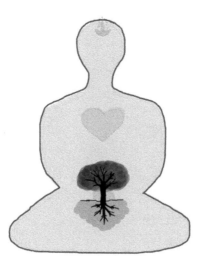

Freeing from the Slave Trade
Restoring the Inner Sovereign
Dissolving in the Gaia

Standing at the final threshold, we now long to reclaim our inner source of power. However, the wounded masculine energy within us gets stuck in a power game. We either hoard and control all power to exploit others. Or, we give away all our power to institutions (governed by the wounded masculine). The rise of new masculine asks men and women to reclaim their true power in service of the whole. This is our final journey to realise the divine masculine.

Power to be Free from institutional slavery: Our journey to realise our full potential is often limited by the institutional and societal roles that we get stuck into. While few men on the top of patriarchal order control all resources, the rest of us trade our authenticity and freedom in exchange for an illusionary sense of safety and inclusion. This is how capitalism, consumerism, religion and all their predecessors kept us stuck in a power(less) game. While we blindly celebrate consumer freedom or communal belonging, like krill, we are simultaneously consumed by a few massive whales of the capitalist power system. To be free, from the influence of this fear-perpetuating machinery, is an essential step to reclaim our power as divine masculine.

Chapter 7, "Freeing from the Slave Trade", highlights the violence created by social institutions and our longing to be free from their power-game.

Power to Rule and honour the inner sovereign: Alpha male (and sometimes female) way of organising collectives has been one of the most prevalent, primitive and suppressive methods. It only worked when the majority gave away its power to one man or woman (the alpha). Disillusioned by the corrupt power structures, many men are leaving the traditional institutions. Some of these enterprising institutional rebels are creating a new distributed economy with rise in freelancers and start-ups. However, they are leaving behind a leadership void in the institutions they worked for. And they are still struggling to organise their own collectives to balance power. The new world demands a revolution of consciousness. It asks all of us to own our power. To awaken our inner sovereign. And co-create a new, awareness-based, institutional paradigm.

Chapter 8, "Restoring the Inner Sovereign", names the leadership void and calls upon men to reclaim their sovereign power.

Power to Dissolve and merge in the Gaia: As we restore the inner King, it is essential to remember the Great Mother (Gaia), we all come from. We are children of the earth, and in her, we dissolve. This awareness frees the masculine from the burden of mindlessly building and resisting nature. Feminine knows this principle of dissolving better as she is more connected to the earth. Reclaiming the power to rule and becoming the King is often misunderstood as the end of the masculine journey. This is precisely where the shadow side of power shows up. It quickly corrupts the powerful and reinforces the old power game, often ending with the suffix '-achy'. Imagine, men at the helm of power-centres who refuse to retire, or, institutions who keep celebrating 150 + years of existence while killing us with sugar and chemicals. They all are stuck, not knowing how to dissolve their ego, and themselves, in service of the ecosystem. Once masculine embraces the power to dissolve, mankind's war with nature and each other is resolved instantaneously.

Chapter 9, "Dissolving in the Gaia", completes the journey to new masculine by exploring the mystical, feminine power to dissolve.

At the end of the threshold of power, we are gifted with self-empowerment. We can see through the institutional power games and know how to be free. We have reclaimed our inner sovereign and understand what it takes to serve our kingdoms. We have surrendered to the great mother, Gaia, and know when to let-go our egos in service of the whole ecosystem.

7

Freeing from the Slave Trade

For long men have been prisoners
Of their own structures
Trading their freedom for an illusionary dream
Turning themselves into a fear-perpetuating machine

He has found his authentic core
And burnt the contract that robbed his soul

Liberated from any shame or guilt
He soars again!

Economy of Inauthenticity

The more I want to live authentic,
More I find myself tied up in ropes of old—
Old promises, old beliefs, old masks, old relationships
All of them painstakingly woven by me
Or traded with others
In the market of social expectations—
   "Why don't you do 30% inauthentic in exchange for the 40%
   I did for you at the wedding!"

Slowly, I got myself deep into the economy of inauthenticity
Trading parts of self for momentary peace and security
Or letting extortion happen
At the gunpoint of nuisance and guilt
Till I was left with the last nickel
The core of my being
My creative self!

I have hidden him for long
Feeling ashamed, possessive, unsure
While all he wants is to be free, from within
Tearing off all the clothes of civilisation
And make-ups of appropriateness

Burning all facades of classes and flags of masses
Ridiculing and laughing at all capitalist' noble purposes—
"How can you save the outer world
when the one inside you is shrinking?"

As he beats in my veins, threatening to explode
I become aware of the web of ropes I am tied into
Nailed to my ribs and hooked with all others around
Unhooking is unbearable, collective pain
"Stay there, wherever you are,
even if it's 80% inauthentic!"

To honour my creative self
I must unhook
I have to bear the pain as one last price of my slavery
I must leave my clothes here
And walk naked

In the economy of inauthenticity
I choose to lose

Unconscious Script of Violence

Waking up in a hotel room somewhere in Africa
Chilled morning breeze across the mountains
Bringing the news of lost humanity

200 girls kidnapped in the name of religion,
47 students killed for claiming their right for the land,
11 journalist jailed for free speech,
More than half the people I see around live in extreme poverty

This is my world too
My mother was born here 3 million years ago,
My ancestors hunted here,
Their wisdom lives in every cell of mine.
My friend studied in the same college where others were killed
I am afraid why is he not responding to my messages

What makes a human so desperate to kill another?

Feeling deep sadness
Tears welling up in my eyes
Fire beneath
Now settling into a heavy warm breath
I close my eyes in meditation
Pictures of violence run in my mind like a mute movie

Camera zooms on the victim
A moment before he lost his life
Camera zooms on the assassinator
A moment before he saw a life lost
Both fearful, both shocked, both seeking forgiveness
One dies. Other is destroyed
One falls on the ground. Other falls in his own eyes
Both are helpless characters of the same script
Unconsciously being written by you and me

Camera zooms on the witness
Fearful, helpless, shocked eyes
I see my face
Sound of Tibetan bell ringing
Compassion wells up from depths of my heart
Words break open from my mouth
"May we all be liberated
from this unconscious script of violence"

Divine Tug of War

Humanity stands at a new threshold
Rising hatred, sinking hope
For every spark of violence
Let's rain a million drops of love

Just before the dawn of new
A massive wave hit our hearts
A relapse of sorts
Intense tribal fear kicked in again
The world started walking backwards
Sliding back into our caves
Of nationality, class, religion or race
Dressed in fear, we stand at the threshold
Will we step out and embrace evolution?
Or further, step in and reinforce separation?

The wall that's built to protect
Isolates and stifles the one within
The gun that's fired to eliminate
Eventually kills the one who holds it
The hatred that justifies righteousness
Often self-sacrifices its proud owner

Once again, we are in a divine tug of war
A manthan within every heart

What would sustain us?
Who will we be at the other end?
What will we tell our children?

Calling Out the Archaic Game of Terror

Animal world predators knew this game well—
First, find a herd, busy feeding their individual selves,
Take them by surprise,
So they run helter-skelter to save their lives
Give an overwhelming dose of fear
Before they get to reflect and organise
Create a scene that disconnects them
From their own power—personal or collective
Find a scapegoat. Slay it.
And feed on it in front of their tribe
Let them ingrain it in their DNA that they are alone,
Fragmented and fragile
Let the fear get hardwired as collective genes
While the predators thrive

* * *

Old world dictators also played it well—
They invented gladiators and wars
And forced the best of their warriors to play a death game
While the rest of the population cheered the public killing
Their inner warrior and their soul was brutally murdered
And amid those celebrations, fear prevailed
Leaving each of the audience, more fragmented and powerless
Finding refuge in the corrupt power-heads

* * *

In the new world, the game became sophisticated
Predators colonised our mind-space
And put us on war against our own-selves
Cancerous capitalist dream, hate politics, soulless media
Co-produced the old terror
And kept masses isolated from their true power

Either way, the game continues
Predator strategies have not changed
Fear remains a valuable currency of power
Free-spirited souls are scapegoated brutally
In front of their mute brothers

* * *

Patterns repeat and will do so unless
We stop and look straight in the eyes of fear
Stand shoulder-to-shoulder, paw the ground and
Let the dirt fly backwards

No lion worth its salt will dare exploit a herd
That stands its ground
No dictator however brutal can thrive
If the audience stands with the gladiator
And calls the game over
No act of terrorism can sustain
If we refuse to feed on its core values
Of fear and fragmentation

No capitalist system can govern our free-spirit
If we refuse to feed our egos from its hands

* * *

When the victim drops his costume of fear,
The oppressor is liberated from his spell of violence
A warrior who has found his inner king
Wins without lifting the sword

In the Market of Emotions

Why insults don't have an expiry date
And kindness is so perishable

Why compliments don't come
With a Best Before Date
And gratitude goes so quickly
Off the shelf

Why fear is produced
At economies of scale
And hope is mined secretly
In far off depths

Why is anger recycled
Or sadness reused

Why not laughter be
Free for all
And love be
A global right!

8

Restoring the Inner Sovereign

Dethroned, wounded, disillusioned
He walked lonely through the dark forests
Till destiny encountered him
With a deserted palace, longing for redemption

Inch by inch, he gathered his force
Reclaiming power
Restoring sovereignty
And calling forth a new world order

In service of the earth and all its being
He rules again!

The Ship that Weathered the Storm

I wake up on a small island
Broken raft rocking gently on the subtle waves
A fleeting lullaby of a failed expedition

Our monotony is disrupted
By a call from the mother ship
I float on my back to her belly

A big mast stands on her wet deck
Steep spiral stairway rising up to the sky
With prayer flags fluttering down like old leaves

I know instantly, the ship has weathered a storm
Something is lost
Something new is awaited

Mother (ship) speaks from her depth—
We had to let go of the old commander
His outburst was unbearable to the mermaids

We will regain our old love affair with the sea
The joy of floating with her limitless being

My crew arrives on a boat
An enigmatic Pirate King climbs the deck
He senses I need time with mother and waits

We stand together
At the helm
Looking at the far, far horizon

His-Story

That night, only I knew
That he would come again

A memory frozen in Middle Ages
A fierce patriarch who ruled our world
Now romanticised in history
Or despised in her-story
Yet, the vividness of his void
Is felt by both kinds

When he showed up again
Hell broke loose
Neither men nor women knew
How to embrace him
The throne that lied unoccupied
Had its master revisiting
A longing that everyone had
But none admitted

He walked swiftly through the mist
A commander, a sovereign
Fearless and focussed
Instantly aligning heaven and earth
Merely with his presence

He gave me a bag
And asked me to open only when I could wear it
It has power and wisdom
Cultivated by his kind for ages
We need it now to sort our mess
And serve the Earth

He, then, dissolved in the fog
The bag I sense has a sovereign order
It's lying unopened on the throne
While we are busy writing history essays
Over pros and cons of his style

Return of the King[11]

On the eve of my enthronement
I fled the Kingdom

I was old enough to know
That the world out there is suffering
I was wise enough to choose
Not to be a perpetrator
I was bold enough to refuse
A throne build on people's painful shoulders
But, I was not clear enough, to know
What next?

Out there, on the edges of civilisation
I joined a company of men called Rangers
Wild and courageous
Defenders of essence
Seers of future
Lovers of earth
Driven by a purpose,
Bigger than any King could hold

---

11 Title & theme of this poem is inspired by the movie The
    Lord of the Rings: The Return of the King. Directed by Peter
    Jackson (2003)

As Rangers, you serve many kingdoms
You challenge the status quo
You wander the whole earth
But you can't own anything
Not even the responsibility of your kingdom

Being at the edges,
Your awareness of others pain
Of nearing death
Gets so acute and real
That, your inability to shift the system
Frustrates you, like never before
That's when a thought creeps in your heart
"Ah, if I was a King"

And that's when,
A messenger from the other world, shows up
With a sword that you were to own
A sword that you thought was broken
A sword that no one other than the King of the land
Can lift to its full glory

The messenger shows up with your sword and a response
"Indeed you are the King"
And it's time for you to return!

Buddha as in You

Just before the first ray of sunlight,
Broke the profound darkness of the night
He was there!

Like a lotus emerging in a swamp
Giving the mess, its long due meaning
Sitting next to me
Breathing freshness of the morning lake
With fading moonlight and glowing dawn
He was there!

He looked at my mess
and asked me to 'stay there'
and till the last ounce of my life
"pour love",

Every night,
Walking miles across the rocky desert
To the little plant of hope
I poured all that I had,
Love!

One day, a flower bloomed
Before I could celebrate, he warned—
Your journey continues
At times you would fail
Flowers too wither
Forests are born long after many nights of spillover

One night, as we were sitting in quiet,
I asked him—
Who are you?

He kept looking at a small path across the jungle
Sun and moon were merging in the sky
Reflecting their shadows in lake
One swan stretched its wing, ready to fly

He smiled as he got up—
"These days you call me Buddha"
"Buddha as in Buddhism"—I exclaimed
"No, Buddha as in you!"—he replied
and dissolved with the moonlight

Naked King

I feel the earth beneath my feet
A momentary chill of her surface and warmth of her core
As my roots find their way to the source
In this very moment, I am grounded
Grateful for her gravity and nourishment
This is the only time and space I truly own
And it's over with every passing moment
So brief is my kingdom
Yet so real and so full

I feel my seat and my back
Strength of my naked spine
And million sacred threads fluttering from my backbone
Reminding me of those who paved this path for me
Grateful to their spirit and grace
This is the only heritage that I have
And it seeks nothing from me
So free is my flow
Yet so solid and so generous

I feel my naked open chest
Tenderness of a broken heart
And natural confidence of broad shoulders
Arms ready to hold and heal the world
Grateful to my wounds for they taught me love
This is the only gift I have
And it's endless
So spacious is my being
Yet so ordinary

I feel the space above my head
Empty limitless sky
Vibrating sound of nothingness
Expanding my being and dissolving in the whole
Grateful for this interconnected awareness
This is the only wisdom I have
And it's never mine
So timeless, so elusive
Yet so present

9

Dissolving in the Gaia

His is a story of survival
A perpetual war against nature
A wounded exile from Eden

He surrendered to Gaia
Letting the old wounds heal
Seeing the whole world within
Celebrating his piece in the grand puzzle

Like an ink-drop in the endless sea
He dissolves again!

Bleeding is Okay

Pick up your lamp
Step out
Smell the rural air

Follow the music
The women dancing
In red and yellow

Sit in the centre
By the alter
Others will join

Wait for your turn
Offer your heart
To the divine

Bleeding is okay
Wounds are openings
The golden heart will be restored

Flowers that Served the Ceremony

All beginnings come to an end
All ends are preceded by
significant middles

The flowers that served the ceremony,
will now serve the field
The roses that centred the living,
will now manure the next
Ever noticed,
the magnificence of endings?

Significance is in knowing,
How to serve the whole

Beauty is being in the place
That needs you

Endings are beginnings
All in the middle of
The great cosmic evolution

Mess is a Mandala

Lost in thick, green, wet woods
Strolling downhill
In search of a space to meditate

What looked like a dead-end
Is threshold for a thicker, darker jungle
Mind rebels, feet walk right across
Not a place inviting enough
Amidst crawling creatures, cobwebs and thorny shrubs
How could anyone find salvation here?

As I drop the plan and turn back
A meadow suddenly shows itself
It was always there, waiting
A pile of stone sits in the centre like a sage
With neatly cut logs inviting me to meditate
But, my legs walk past that too

An old fallen tree
At the edge of a quiet lake
Whispers my name

As I settle, the whole design falls in place

That lost path was a pilgrimage,
I was unaware of

This mess is a mandala,
A work of art

I am the missing puzzle piece,
I was looking for!

Walking on Water

With every step I take,
There are ripples

And as I step in,
They turn into a floating petal

As I lift my foot
The petal dissolves in the water

Something in this vast blue ocean is mine
Dissolved yet unique!
Dissolved yet unique!

When it Resolves, it Dissolves

Whatever seeks resolution within
Whatever is stuck, unhealthy, unhealed,
Whatever is hurt, not understood, not honoured
What so ever that is…

It's a product of "I" not in resonance with the whole
The ego not in rhythm with the collective
The disturbance not connected with the essence

Eventually, at its own will, in its own time
It will dissolve,
The I in we
The other in me
The gross in subtle

Anitya . Anitya . Anitya[12].

---

12   Anitya = Sanskrit for impermanence

At this stage of our journey, we sit in silence with a solid back and an open heart. We feel the divine masculine and divine feminine integrating within us. Our past is metabolised into wisdom coming from ages. Our deep wounds are healed into compassion. And, our spirit is rising to stand and serve.

Integration

At the Dawn of His Coronation
He Rises Again
Design Your Own Journey

At the Dawn of His Coronation

Standing on two feet, fearless and real
Spine straight, gaze resting in clarity
Heart open, embracing the whole
Back still healing, from the long night of war

At the crack of the new dawn, on his coronation,
He celebrates the communion with his soul,
His woman, his child and his kingdom

To self,
He has visited old shames and deep wounds
They have not healed yet
But he has learnt to dance with his dark
Rooted in his essence
Shameless, vulnerable and strong
He stands!

To his inner woman,
He has slaughtered his own chariot—
the monstrous ride of patriarchy
And burnt the million scared threads
of expectations, shoulds, norms and forms
His energy fiercely available again
To rise in love...

Pure, naked and authentic
He stands!

To his inner child,
He has touched his innocence
That tender purity vibrating beneath his ribs
He dissolved all masks that held him away from himself
Playful, gentle, protective,
For his inner child and children of the world
He stands!

To the institutions,
who prisoned his free spirit
He has resigned
Unplugged from the unspoken slavery
of convenience, fear, desires
He sees what matters and fiercely attends
He is raising a new war for reclaiming humanity
He stands!

Sit with him, and you will feel his kingdom
in his presence, grace and honour
Sit with him, and you feel your kingdom
in his presence, grace and honour

He Rises Again!

Is he really new?
Or a return to the,
—very, very primordial man within?
Natives, as old as, the earth
Knew this forever

At his core, he is whole
Dancing starlight of
Divine feminine and divine masculine
Landing on earth like a seed
Vulnerable and unique
Holding the blueprint of the whole forest
—a raw, unapologetic humanity

He will sprout
A part rising to meet the sky
Other deepening to touch the source
From Her very essence
He rises again!

Design Your Own Journey – Reader's Guide

What if you could design your personal pathway to heal the wounded masculine within you and unleash your gifts of freedom, love and power?

Proposing a design framework is in the realm of researchers and theorists. They gather experiential data, identify patterns and propose a framework. Poets, on the other hand, inspire, mirror, invoke and evoke profound experiences. But they seldom structure experiences into a framework.

Yet, poetry is a deep inquiry. Poets explore existential questions with the rigour of micro-phenomenology. Unlike researchers, we may not start with a specific question or hypothesis. But we do access the deep sense of unrest that lies below any inquiry. Its both personal and systemic. In a way, poets, like researchers, tend to uncover the deeper archetypal patterns of life.

The kaleidoscope of the new masculine has endless patterns. What I have offered in this book is just one. However, I can translate my creative impulses and frustrations into questions that may guide your exploration. I hope these questions give you the nudge to take your inner journey. Treat them like your guides. Take them for a walk in the woods. Or let them stare at your naked self from the foggy mirror. If they open up new questions or trigger old memories, follow that thread. When you come back, write. That's your pathway in the making.

Introduction: Preparing for the Journey

Where in your life do you feel most misunderstood as a man? Or as a woman, what part of your masculine energy frustrates you the most?

What are the armours of masculinity or manhood you were born into? What roles, assumptions, values about the same frustrate you the most?

The Threshold of Knowledge
Overcoming Past Conditionings

Take a moment to reconnect with the life stories of your parents, grandparents and your tribe. What were the key life choices and struggles that they went through? If it was a movie, what would you name it? Where is your life becoming a sequel of the same? What part of this story you do not want to carry any more?

What aspect of your inner person you haven't touched yet? What are you most dreadful of within yourself?

What is your relationship with anger or rage? What makes you feel sad and hurt? If you let yourself feel these emotions fully, what would they say?

The Threshold of Love
Healing Deep Wounds

Reflect on your most intimate conflicts. These may be unresolved struggles with your partner or parents. If it was a duet, what song are you singing? What are you both longing for?

What part of your sexuality feels repressed and locked away? If that part had a shape, a colour, a being, a voice—what would it look like?

Take a quiet walk down the memory lane to your childhood. Is there a part of your childhood you haven't met in a while? How does that little one feel?

The Threshold of Power
Reclaiming Inner Sources

If you were a bird, what is the cage or net you are stuck into? What are the webs of institutional roles, societal expectations, fears and cravings that bind you from expressing your true self? What would this bird cry for?

Connect with the part of you that has abandoned the throne. Where in life, you most struggle with power? What is the kingdom that's longing for you to return?

Spend some quiet time speaking with Mother Earth. What would she advise you about your journey? What do you need to fully surrender or dissolve?

Integration

Imagine yourself at the end of your journey. You are walking into a castle that's situated in depths of your heart. It's the day of your coronation. Greet and connect with all the people or images you come across. Now walk to the inner sanctum in sovereign presence of a King, a Queen, a Child and a Minister. How would they celebrate you? What would you say?

About the Author

Manish Srivastava wrote his first poem at the age of nine. But after he discovered his divine gift, his life got divided into two roads.

The upper road took the course of his professional life. He learnt his ropes in defence, business and international development sectors and found his way to the renowned institutions of Harvard, MIT, Unilever etc.

However, his soul found refuge in the down road—a less celebrated path of poetry, art and nature. It was here he made sense of the crazy demanding world and engaged in authentic self-inquiry through dream analysis and contemplative art.

Somewhere down the line, two roads crossed. Manish now works as a life-coach and consultant with leaders across international governments, MNCs, social enterprises, grassroots women networks and men circles. He integrates contemplative arts, depth psychology and systems thinking to facilitate deep dialogue on sustainability challenges like mental well-being, women empowerment, anti-trafficking, climate change, social justice, youth etc.

Manish is a core faculty of Social Presencing Theatre with Presencing Institute, USA. He lives in Pune, India with his wife and son.

Manish explores deeper aspects of humanity through poems and essays, on themes of deep masculine, feminine, relationships, collective healing, eco-sustainability and leadership; on his blog: www.sacredwell.in

To share your reflections on this book and engage in the emerging movement of the new masculine, follow Manish Srivastava on:

facebook.com/authormanishsrivastava
instagram.com/poetmanish

Lightning Source UK Ltd.
Milton Keynes UK
UKHW012124250620
365566UK00003B/634